CW01424557

the
linde werdelin
ski guide

SWITZERLAND

Beautiful
Books

We are both keen freeskiers. Growing up in Denmark, we have been skiing together in the Alps since the age of six. Over the years, we have built our knowledge of the best runs, hotels and restaurants in each resort and have put this guide book together to share our experiences of skiing and the mountain lifestyle with you.

In 2006, we produced the first ski guide book for Switzerland, since then we have expanded the range to include France and Italy. We will be updating and expanding the guide books each year, as we continue to find new gems, to provide you with the first hand information you need to experience superior skiing.

Our passion for skiing was one of the inspirations behind the founding of LINDE WERDELIN in 2002 and we hope that you too will find inspiration through the exploration of the peaks and valleys of the alps; you may even find a hidden gem even we do not know of.

We hope you have excellent skiing conditions and enjoy this season.

OUR COMMANDMENTS

1. Always plan ahead, always place safety first and wear top quality equipment.

2. Remember to wear an avalanche beacon – always – and know how to use it. There is no good reason not to. Also make sure your skiing partner knows how to use it otherwise it's not much help for you.

3. Never ski outside the marked areas without a guide – it is just not worth the risk however harmless it looks. Besides, a good mountain guide makes everything worth skiing better.

4. When you ski with a guide only share the day with another three friends. Too many people slows the day down and limits the guide's ability to guide.

5. Always make sure your skis are properly serviced and waxed with sharp edges (87-88 degrees for steep and hard skiing). Too often people think it is extravagant to spend CHF 50/€ 30 for an overnight service when they wouldn't think twice about spending this on a starter!

6. Make sure you are properly hydrated in the morning and throughout the day. You will feel much fresher and stronger when skiing.

7. Check the weather (eg: barometer trend) in the

morning to avoid any nasty surprises. It will help you plan your day – and decide whether to book for lunch inside or outside.

8. Boots, skis and other equipment in general should be as good as you expect your skiing to be. We have found that skis keep for 100-150 days of skiing or a maximum of 3 years; and boots 150-200 days or 5 years max. It makes a tremendous difference to your enjoyment and safety to have tight fitting boots and skis that match your skills, weight and

style – most people underestimate the importance of skis.

9. To master your skiing it's best to divide your time over the season, don't go only once – go for a weekend, a week, a few days or longer if you can! Otherwise you may not get the fantastic days that you will remember.

10. Have fun!

SAINT MORITZ

St. Moritz has been a privileged playground ever since it inaugurated winter tourism almost 150 years ago. It is situated in the beautiful Engadine Valley and offers skiing on a variety of mountains right from the town as well as in surrounding areas.

This is not your typical cute mountain village like Zermatt, but rather a town of grandiose stately hotels, Michelin Guide eateries and a luxurious lifestyle.

Few ski aficionados can afford St. Moritz, so this is a spot where the powder often stays untouched for days.

SURROUNDINGS

Corviglia (3,055 m)

The Corviglia is the most convenient ski area, located right in the centre of town.

There are a handful of advanced couloirs on the back side of the Piz Nair. They are among the most difficult fare in this area.

Corvatsch (3,305 m)

We like Corvatsch best among the different mountains in St. Moritz. Most glaciers are gentle, but the tongue of the Corvatsch Glacier has a gradient of about 40 degrees. If that is not enough to get your adrenaline flowing then try a descent down the Furtschellas Couloir, which is a little steeper still and much narrower.

A great way to finish the day is with a run down the black Hahnensee run back to St. Moritz, where the skiing is excellent and not too difficult and the views of the lakes below are a bonus.

Lagalb (2,960 m)

The mountain has only one cable car, but that is enough to offer some excellent skiing, and rarely are there many people on the slopes here.

If, through some quirk of fate, the slopes are more crowded than usual, drop off the back of the mountain and try the Tour La Rosa for great off-piste skiing and pure solitude. This route is difficult to find without a guide.

Diavolezza (2,980 m)

The Diavolezza ski area offers a rather easy but picturesque and worthwhile ungroomed route over the Diavolezza-Morteratsch Glacier. While this attracts the tourists, hardly anybody skis the much more challenging off-piste route down the Val Arias on the other side of the cable car.

The length and dates of the season vary depending on the specific mountain and can be altered year on year depending on weather conditions, as a general rule though, access to the mountains is as follows:
Corvigilia: mid-November until mid-April.
Corvatsch: mid-November until early May.
Diavolezza/Lagalb: mid-September until mid-November, then; mid-December until late-May.

MOUNTAINS

MOUNTAIN GUIDES

Suvretta Snowsports St. Moritz

A member of Prada's Leading Ski Schools and one of the best ski schools in Switzerland. Book a private mountain tour and tailor the programme to your own objectives.

+41 (0)81 836 61 61   www.suvrettasnowsports.ch

Piz Palü
3905 m
Piz Bernina
4049 m
Piz Scerscen
3971 m
Piz Roseg
3937 m
Piz Murtèl
3433 m
Piz Cambrena
3604 m
Piz Legalb
2959 m
Poschiavo,
Tirano
Lagalb, 2893 m
Sass Queder
3066 m
Diavolezza, 2978 m
Alp Grüm
2091 m
Munt Pers
3207 m
Lago Bianco
2234 m
Val Arlas
Bernina Bahn
Morteratschgletscher
Lej da Vadret
Bernina Lagalb, 2107 m
Bernina-Diavolezza, 2093 m
Piz Chalchagn
3154 m
Val Roseg
Gand' Alva, 2643 m
Stüvetta Margun, 2497 m
Corvatsch Surlej, 1870 m
Piz Languard
3262 m
Morteratsch, 1896 m
Champfèr
Suvretta, 1900 m
Chasellas
Alp Languard, 2330 m
St. Moritz Bad, 1772 m
PONTRESINA, 1805 m
ENGADIN
St.Moritz
Muottas Muragl, 2456 m
visiorama
visiorama.ch
A. Rohweder
8/2008

Piz Tremoggia 3441 m
Piz Fora 3363 m
Piz de la Margna 3159 m
Monte Sissone 3330 m
Piz Badile 3308 m

...en, 2600 m
Crap Melan
Furtschellas La Chüdera, 2312 m
L'vu da Segl
Segl-Maria, 1809 m
Furtschellas, 1797 m
Piz Aela 2159 m
Lej da Cavloc 1907 m
Passo del Maloja e 1815 m
Maloja, 1809 m
Piz Lunghin 2780 m
Piz Grevasalvas 2932 m
Lago da l'Albigna 1907 m
Soglio, 1096 m
Bergell
Chiavenna, Milano
Piz Platta 3392 m

Piz Laurev 3194 m

Piz Güglia Piz Julier 3380 m
Pass dal Güglia Julierpass 2284 m
Brüll, 1703 m
Piz d'Err 3378 m
Piz Ela, 3339 m
Corn da Tinzong, 3172 m
Tiefencastel Chur, Zürich

Puercia Grischa
Foch
Les Trais Fluors, 2753 m
Preda, 1789 m
Giline
Marguns, 2273 m
Pass d'Alvra Albulapass 2312 m
Piz Kesch / Piz d'Escha 3418 m
Bergün, 1373 m
Filisur, 1032 m
Vaduz
Tiefencastel Chur, Zürich
Davos, Klosters

Spinas, 1815 m
Pizzet, 2465 m
Albanas, 2360 m
Piz Vadret, 3229 m
Piz Sarsura, 3178 m

120 m
Samedan, 1706 m
Bever, 1711 m
Pulpi, 1697 m
Madulain, 1697 m
Chasellatsch
Crasta
Sovlih
Chamues-ch, 1706 m
Zuoz, 1716 m
S-chanf, 1669 m
Cinous-chel, 1613 m
Bugls
Brail, 1623 m
Zernez, 1471 m
Ofenpass, Münstertal
Scuol Landeck

RESTAURANTS

MOUNTAIN RESTAURANTS
The Chasellas
Based low on the Corvatsch slopes, just above Champfer and visible from hotel Suvretta, the Chasellas is one of the most ambitious mountain restaurants in St. Moritz. It serves traditional Swiss and international food. Try the Wiener Schnitzel and, if you are lucky and they have it, the Apfelstrüdel. It is an excellent meeting point with a nice sun terrace with good shelter from the wind. Although it can be hard to get a table during rush hour.
+41 (0)81 833 38 54

Chesa Chantarella
High above St. Moritz on the Engadin plateau, Chesa Chantarella offers excellent traditional food and a nice, warm interior. They also have an excellent wine cellar boasting 550 different varieties, with tours and tastings available.
10 Via Salastrains, CH-7500   +41 (0)81 833 33 55

El Paradiso
Described as Switzerland's 'finest ski hut' it has both simple traditional and international food served in a trendy but traditional environment each day for lunch. Cosy up on the terrace with sheepskin covered sun beds and enjoy the breathtaking panoramic views; a fantastic place to relax for a couple of hours.
The restaurant will pick you up by Snow Cat from

Salastrains and bring you back to the same spot after your gourmet dinner.

Via Engiadina / Randolins, CH 7500   +41 (0)81 833 40 02

Bergrestaurant Trutz

Suvretta House's mountain lodge on the Corvatsch slopes; fantastic views and hearty food – try their local tortellini followed by Kaiserschmarrn – ideal skiing food.

+41 (0)81 833 70 30

RESTAURANTS IN TOWN
If you like fine cuisine, your palate will be well served as St. Moritz boasts seven Michelin stars and 341 Gault & Millau points.

Jöhri's Talvo
Owned and run by Brigitte and Roland Jöhri who pride themselves on their combination of fine cuisine and welcoming atmosphere - the Talvo also has its own range of deli products and recipe books so you can try your hand at home. Housed in a fine old farmhouse at Champfer, just outside town. Two Michelin stars.
15 via Gunels, CH-7512, St. Moritz-Champfèr
+41 (0)81 833 44 55

Chesa Veglia
An outpost of Badrutt's it's an ancient farmhouse (a couple of minutes away) with three smooth restaurants - the Pizzeria for original Italian pizzas and pasta, the Grill room Chadafö for elegant dining with classic French cuisine and the Patrizier Stuben for Swiss and international specialities.
It is noted its style as much as its food.
Badrutt's Palace Hotel, 27 via Serlas, CH-7500
+41 (0)81 837 26 70

Nobu
Sister restaurant to the renowned Nobu London, is an excellent Japanese place in Badrutt's. Legendary

dishes such as Tiradito, Black Cod with Miso and New Style Sashimi, among others, are available on the Nobu à la carte menu.
Badrutt's Palace Hotel, 27 via Serlas, CH-7500
+41 (0)81 837 26 70

Chesa Pirani

At La Punt a few kilometres down the valley in a charming old house with panelled rooms. It also has two Michelin stars. Also known as Bumanns, after its famous chef-proprietor.
Bumanns Chesa Pirani, CH-7522, La Punt near St. Moritz
+41 (0)81 854 25 15

Grischuna

The elegantly furnished interior is completed wonderfully by chef Jens Nardmann's excellent Italian food, while Marco Losi works to provide a relaxing dining experience. Located in the Hotel Monopol.
Hotel Monopol, 17 via Maistra, CH-7500   +41 (0)81 837 04 04

Chesa Dorta

An old Engadin farmhouse a few miles north of St. Moritz in Zuoz.
Serves traditional Grison specialities.
Chesa Dorta, CH-7524, Zuoz   +41 (0)81 854 20 40

APRÈS-SKI

King's Club

An upscale grown-up nightclub ("no curfew") in Badrutt's Palace.

Guest DJs and regular themed nights add to the sheer decadence of the experience.

27 via Serlas, CH-7500   +41 (0)81 837 26 70

Dracula's Ghost Riders Club

A private members' club (in theory). Orignially founded in 1972 by Gunther Sachs as a place to hang out with his friends, the club has retained this friendly vibe while also rising to become one of the places to be seen in St. Moritz.

54 via Maistra, CH-7500   +41 (0)81 833 2020

Pavarotti & Friends

In the so-called 'downtown' this cosy bar has good tapas and great wine. If you are lucky the owner will sing operatic arias.

3 plazza dal Mulin, CH-7500   +41 (0)81 833 07 00

Bodega

Spanish wine and over thirty possible combinations of tapas, Bodega is found in a rustic old cellar beneath Hotel Misani.

Hotel Misani, CH-7500, St. Moritz-Celerina
+41 (0)81 839 89 89

Rote Bar

Cool, architect-designed bar in Hotel Castell at Zuoz. For a relaxed evening drop in for 'Blue Hour', an evening of lounge music, every evening between five and seven.

Hotel Castell, CH-7524, Zuoz   +41 (0)81 851 52 53

Cascade

Trendy restaurant and bar, with a Jugendstil interior, which has become a meeting point for both locals and tourists under the management of Daniel Müller. Local and Italian cuisine and a good spot for an aperitif or cocktail.

6 via Somplaz 6, CH-7500   +41 (0)81 833 33 44

HOTELS

St. Moritz has Switzerland's greatest concentration of five-star hotels. A five-star hotel in St. Moritz would qualify as a 6-star anywhere else. In addition, these hotels are full of 19 th century atmosphere. All have grand public rooms, multiple restaurants and of course superb facilities. Some of the restaurants have a dress code so bring a suit and a tie.

Carlton Hotel

After an extensive refurbishment programme in 2007 the Carlton is the first luxury boutique hotel in St. Moritz. The colourful all-suite hotel redefines luxury providing a personal and attentive service in a private and intimate surrounding.

Carlton Hotel, CH-7500

+41 (0)81 836 70 00   www.carlton-stmoritz.ch

Hotel Castell

A multi-award winning hotel in Zuoz, the Hotel Castell is an exciting blend of turn-of-the-century rooms with modern architecture and art, a fashionable contrast that has not diminished the hospitality of Bettina and Richard Plattner-Gerber, the dedicated hoteliers. The hotel also hosts items from the Walther A. Bechtler Foundation as well as an extensive library and media collection on the contemporary at scene.

Hotel Castell, CH-7524 Zuoz

+41 (0)81 851 52 53   www.hotelcastell.ch

Suvretta House

Is where we prefer to stay. It is at a secluded out-of-town location at the foot of the pistes (ski-in, ski-out). You will always feel at home here with their very attentive and personal service. All facilities are excellent.

1 via Chasellas, CH-7500

+41 (0)81 836 36 36   www.suvrettahouse.ch

Laudinella

An innovative modern hotel down in Bad with multiple varied restaurants. No trace of traditional Alpine style.

17 via Tegiatscha, CH-7500

+41 (0)81 836 00 00   www.laudinella.ch

Kulm

The hotel where Johannes Badrutt started it all just over 150 years ago; it's still the Cresta Run riders' base. Very traditional and comfortable. Located in the shopping area.

Kulm Hotel St. Moritz, CH-7500

+41 (0)81 836 80 00   www.kulmhotel-stmoritz.ch

Badrutt's Palace

Part of St. Moritz's history, started in 1892 by Johannes' son Caspar Badrutt. It has a traditional style with everything (plus more) you can expect from a five-star hotel including 7 restaurants, 4 bars and 2 clubs. It is located in the main shopping area and attracts a jet-set après-ski crowd.

27 via Serlas, CH-7500
+41 (0)81 837 10 00   www.badruttspalace.com

THINGS TO DO

Shopping

Every top name in the world of high fashion is represented here, including Gucci, Bally, Hermès, Chanel, Louis Vuitton, Roberto Cavalli, ETRO and many, many more; a stroll down the Via Serlas is like a 'who's who' of luxury fashion.

Cresta Run

This 1,100 m long, balls-to-the-wall proof of manhood has almost as long a tradition as the skiing here, having been inaugurated in 1887. This is a run down an icy track on a small skeleton toboggan that is ridden lying on ones stomach head first at speeds that get up to 125 km/h. If you remain on board through the entire ride, including the infamous Shuttlecock Bend, you have truly accomplished something and deserve a bottle of champagne in the King's Club under the Palace Hotel. The run is generally open to men only from just before Christmas until the end of February.

Other Sports

St. Moritz is situated along the shores of the lovely Lake of St. Moritz. Ever since the British upper class inaugurated winter tourism here in the second half of the 19th century, they brought with them their games and sports. The frozen lake was the perfect venue for those activities. Here, one can view or participate in a number of sports that are generally played only in summer, including polo, horse racing, golf and cricket.

White Turf St. Moritz
Various forms of horse racing are on offer including skijöring (skiers pulled by riderless horses). It is held on three Sundays in February.

Night Skiing
Held every Friday during the season on Corvatsch from 8:00 pm to 2:00 am.

Alpine Ski World Cup
This year St. Moritz is hosting the men's slalom event from the 18th to the 19th of December.

The Nietzsche-Haus
Nietzsche's summer retreat from 1881 to 1888, the house now hosts both a permanent exhibition on the man himself and a regular calendar of modern art collections.

Nietzsche-Haus, CH-7514, Sils Maria   +41 (0)81 826 53 69

Segantini Museum
Dedicated to the works of the renowned alpine symbolist painter Giovanni Segantini, the museum opened in 1908 and is based on Segantini's own design for the pavillon that was to be exhibited at the Paris World Exhibition in 1900.

30 via Somplaz, CH-7500   +41 (0)81 833 44 54

The St. Moritz Design Gallery

Housed in the pedestrian walkway between the parking garage of the railway station, the lake and the Palace Hotel, the gallery is divided into 35 sections lined with posters providing a visual history of design.

SPAS AND RELAXATION

MTZ Heilbad St. Moritz

St. Moritz has a long history as a spa town dating back to the fifteenth century, with its waters being used for healing purposes for as long as 3000 years. Today the Heilbad has brought this tradition into the 21st century and can offer all that one might expect from such a rich past combined with modern treatments.

2 plazza Paracelsus, CH-7500

+41 (0)81 833 30 62   www.heilbad-stmoritz.ch

TRAVEL

While St. Moritz may be closer to Milan airport, it is a much simpler prospect to arrive at Zurich and travel from there.

PUBLIC TRANSPORT

The public transport network in Switzerland is excellent, known for its comfort and reliability and is by far the best way to get around.

Train

There is a regular service running from Zurich Hauptbahnhof to St. Moritz; trains leave on an hourly basis with a change at Chur.

www.sbb.ch

Taxi St. Moritz

Should you require a private hire service then Taxi St. Moritz offer a range of services from short haul transfers to international travels.

+41 79 611 13 10   www.taxi-stmoritz.ch

USEFUL CONTACTS

St. Moritz Tourist Information
Tel +41 (0)81 837 33 33
www.engadin.stmoritz.ch/stmoritz

Engadin St. Moritz Mountain Pool
Ski lift and weather information.
Tel +41 (0)81 830 00 00
www.engadin.stmoritz.ch/mountains

EMERGENCY NUMBERS
Oberengadin Hospital   +41 (0)81 851 81 11

VAL D'ANNIVIERS

Val d'Anniviers branches away from the beautiful Rhône Valley and is the most easterly French-speaking valley in Switzerland.

This side valley is home to the little-known ski villages of Vercorin, Chandolin, St. Luc, Grimentz and Zinal, and 220 kilometres of pistes.

These villages cannot and do not try to compete with their famous neighbours in the areas of nightlife and après-ski. But, Val d'Anniviers' lack of notoriety makes it one of our favourite ski areas. The grooming is excellent, the pistes are relatively empty allowing for high-speed cruising, and one can often ski fresh powder for days on end between snowfalls.

Some of the off-piste skiing in Val d'Anniviers is easy to find as virgin powder often lies within plain sight of the lifts, just waiting to be sprayed up into your face.

SURROUNDINGS

Grimentz (1,570 m)

Ancient houses with hundreds of years of sunshine burnt into the wood make Grimentz one of the most picturesque villages in the Alps. It looks like a spot where, at any moment, Heidi will come skipping around the corner with a pail of fresh milk.

To stroll through the village is to wander into the 13th century, the period from which many of the houses originate. Narrow streets wind among antique chalets, barns, cowsheds and storage buildings called Raccards.

The Orzival Lift and the Piste Lona from atop the Lona T-bar provide some challenging runs. From the Orzival

Lift, you can also access a back valley that descends to the hamlet of St. Jean.
The winter season lasts from mid-December until mid-April.

Zinal (1,670 m)

The village of Zinal also has picturesque old wooden houses, although it is not quite as quaint as Grimentz. However, it has the steepest pistes and perhaps the best off-piste skiing in the valley.

In addition, the ski area offers a view of the so-called Imperial Crown – five peaks which all top 4,000 m. The Weisshorn (4,505 m), the Zinalrothorn (4,221 m), the Obergabelhorn (4,063 m), the Dent Blanche (4,357 m)

and the Matterhorn (4,476 m) create an amazing backdrop to the powder paradise here.

Zinal has a dedicated freeride area just a short traverse out from the Combe Durand lift. To access this zone, you should have a shovel and ski partner, as well as an avalanche transceiver… and even your beeper will not open heaven's gate if the avalanche risk is higher than stage two!
For the best runs, ski this all the way to the bottom rather than cutting back to the middle station.

In addition, a 45 minute hike from the freeride zone traverse brings energetic freeriders past the next ridge

and back out of the controlled zone to the Combe de Singlinaz. From there you can embark down a huge face followed by a couloir that leads you on a long thriller back to Zinal.

The open slopes from the highest point in Zinal's lift system, the top of the Corne de Sorebois lift (2,896 m), also provide some easy-to-find powder right after a snowstorm.

Zinal's reputation as a powder pearl, however, derives from a few of the wonderful back-side descents that are not quite so obvious at first glance. One of these back valley runs is the Piste du Chamois, a long and aptly named North face beginning atop the Corne de Sorebois Lift that takes skiers to Grimentz or to the hamlet of Mottec, between Grimentz and Zinal.

Another fabulous powder run descends the wide west faces behind the Corne de Sorebois to the Lac de Moiry.
You can also ski some even steeper descents to the lake from the top of the Combe Durand Lift. Part way down, you cross a monstrous dam and eventually follow a trail to Grimentz.

Zinal's slopes are open to the public every weekend from early November until mid-December, when they are accessible daily until mid-April.

St. Luc (1,650 m) / Chandolin (1,950 m)

These two villages are also home to some beautiful old Walliser houses. This is the largest lift system in the valley.

The Pas de Bœuf is an excellent long red cruise. Its 1,200 m vertical will certainly challenge anyone trying to ski it non-stop. Like the other villages in the valley, the real treasure here is the off-piste skiing.

One of the best runs here is the Illhorn Couloir, easily accessed from atop the Illhorn T-bar. This gem is close to 40 degrees steep and is followed by open slopes that bring you back around to the bottom of the lift.

There are many couloirs along the Arete des Ombreintses – a ridge that separates St. Luc from Chandolin, but most of these have a gradient of 45 to 50 degrees, making them much more extreme than the Illhorn run.

They are full of rocks as well and have claimed many victims over the years.

The Couloir de Bus, in the middle of the group of chutes is probably the easiest. Even the intrepid should probably test their skills on this one before venturing down any of its more nefarious neighbours, and the judgment and leadership of a mountain guide is imperative on all of these chutes.

Not everything here is narrow and exposed. Like its neighbours, St. Luc has some wonderful wide-open terrain as well. Both the Le Rotse and the Remointze chair lifts bring you to the top of some lovely slopes that are easy to scout and see from the lifts.
They begin above the tree line and finish with some excellent skiing in the forest. There are also some nice open powder fields to be found by traversing about 300 m southwest of the Bella Tola T-bar.

The Bella Tola is also the starting point for one of the best ski tours in the area. A two-and-a-half hour hike on skins brings you to the peak of Le Tounôt. From there, you can dive into a 35 degree chute. Once you have negotiated the chute successfully, a long run to the valley still awaits, and one can add a perfect conclusion to this excursion by finishing it with a lunch at the cozy Le Prilet restaurant a short way up the valley from St. Luc.

Skiing is possible from mid-December until mid-April.

Vercorin (1,322 m)

This is one more postcard-perfect village complete with old wooden houses and Raccards. The runs are not as long and the skiing not as steep here as in the other villages, but in the right conditions, you can find some good tree-skiing here.

Vercorin's slopes are open from mid-December until mid-April.

Weisshorn
4505

Zinalrothorn
4221

Obergabelhorn
4063

Cervin
Matterhorn
4478

Dent Blanche
4357

Dent d'Hérens
4171

Tête Blanche
3724

Cabane
Tracuit

Besso
3668

Grand Cornier
3962

Cabane
du Mountet

Cabane
de Moiry

Cabane
d'Ar Pitetta

Les Diablons
3609

Cabane
Petit Mountet

Combe de Sorebois

Sex Marenda

Le Toûno

Pointe de Tsirouc
2777

Lac
de Moiry

ZINAL

Sorebois

Pointes
de Nava

Bella Tola

MOLTEC

Hôtel Weisshorn

AYER

GRIMENTZ

Bercour
2712

Rothorn

Cabane
Lirec

MISSION

La Brinta

Tsapé
2475

Cabane
Bella Tola

Tignousa

ST-LUC

VISSOIE

PINSEC

Mt Major
3200

Bendolla

Crêt du Midi

Sillen Giez
et Chermeville

Cabane
Veyras

CHANDOLIN

Cabane
Illhorn

SOUSSILLON

Tsapé

Les Chardonnières

Cabane
Tsapé

Cabane
de l'Arpitettaz

Les Pontis

VERCORIN

Chapelle Cornu

Les Tittots

Pôterette

NIOUC

Brey

CHALAIS

RÉCHY

BRIGUE

Forêt de Finges

CHIPPIS

Le Rhône

SIERRE
563

SALGESCH

VEYRAS
MIÈGE
VENTHÔNE

NOES

BRON
ST-LÉ

MOUNTAINS

MOUNTAIN GUIDES
Mountain Reality Bergschule Uri
Has a number of guides who are specialists in this region and Stefan Jossen is perhaps the top specialist for Val d'Anniviers. He is an extremely knowledgeable guide with expedition experience from the Alps to the Himalayas.

+41 (0)41 872 09 00 www.bergschule-uri.ch

EQUIPMENT
Sport 4000
An equipment specialist in St. Luc with sale and rental. They also stock Mammut.

Au vieux village, 3961 St. Luc +41 (0)2 74 75 13 48

RESTAURANTS

MOUNTAIN RESTAURANTS
GRIMENTZ
Bendolla
At the top of the Bendolla gondola.
Regional specialties and Valaisan wines.
+41 (0)27 476 20 15

ZINAL
Restaurant de Sorebois
This high altitude restaurant, situated at 2,440 m, is accessed with the Zinal cable car and has a lovely view of the Imperial Crown from its terrace.
Serves Valaisan specialities and homemade pastries and cakes.
+41 (0)27 475 13 78

CHANDOLIN
Cabane l'Ilhorn
Lovely old stone hut on the slopes, an excellent spot for good mountain food and wine. Last time we were there I had a fantastic 'tarte aux myrtilles'.
+41 (0)27 475 11 78

RESTAURANTS IN TOWN
Crêperie La Versache
A pancake paradise with over 50 varieties.
Also serving viande séchée, a dried spiced meat dish and made to order Gallion fondue.
Crêperie La Versache, 3961 Zinal   +41 (0)27 475 11 69

La Poste Restaurant

Mainly cheese dishes and local specialities. Great for cheese fondue.

Hotel de la Poste, 3961 Zinal   +41 (0)27 475 11 87

Tzambron

At the Grand Hotel Bella Tola in St. Luc offers regional specialities with cheese, fondue, raclette, rösti and a wide selection of wines. Warm ambience.

Hotel Bella Tola, Rue Principale, 3961 St. Luc
+41 (0)27 475 14 44

Le Prilet

Cosy chalet style restaurant worth stopping into. A good finishing point for the Le Touno ski tour.

Gîte du Prilet, 3961 St. Luc   +41 (0)27 475 11 55

APRÈS-SKI

Snow bar Chez Florioz

At the bottom of the Grimentz piste; has a good après-ski atmosphere.

Bar à Neige Chez Florioz, 3961 Grimentz   +41 (0)78 338 70 89

HOTELS

Val d'Anniviers offers a very different style of hotels to St. Moritz and Zermatt. The majority are three and four stars, but most have a certain charm.

GRIMENTZ
Alpina Hotel

A new hotel ideally located at the bottom of the slopes in Grimentz. This chalet style hotel is known for its cuisine and tranquillity.

Hotel Alpina, 3961 Grimentz
+41 (0)27 476 16 16   www.hotel-alpina-grimentz.com

VISSOIE
Hotel Anniviers & Manoir

A Swiss style country house in the heart of the Vissoie village. Comfortable with charm.

Au Manoir d'Anniviers, 3961 Vissoie
+41 (0)27 475 12 20   www.aumanoirdanniviers.ch

ST. LUC
Grand Hotel Bella Tola

Decorated with period furniture, it provides an ambiance of yesteryear and has an excellent kitchen for those who might only come here to enjoy a meal. The outside terrace provides a beautiful view over the valley. We have stayed in the little house facing the main road for extra space (with absolutely no traffic).

Grand Hotel Bella Tola & St. Luc, 3961 St. Luc
+41 (0)27 475 14 44   www.bellatola.ch

Le Beausite

Offers comfort and tranquillity. Authentic cuisine in the café restaurant serving local specialities.
Hotel Le Beausite, 3961 St. Luc
+41 (0)27 475 15 86   www.lebeausite.ch

Weisshorn Hotel

At 2,337 m is slightly isolated but has an impressive panoramic view.
Hotel Weisshorn, 3961 St. Luc
+41 (0)27 475 11 06   www.weisshorn.ch

THINGS TO DO

Free Flight School
Parapente and hang gliding available for beginners and seasoned pros alike in Zinal, all under the watchful eye of Philipe; if you are feeling particularly skilled why not enter the annual Zinal Mauler Cup.
+41 (0)79 447 35 87   www.vol-libre.ch

Rainer Maria Rilke Foundation
Located in the small village of Sierre at the mouth of the valley in the "Pancrace de Courten" house that dates back to 1769, the museum is dedicated to the Prague poet who lived in Veyras from 1921 to 1926.
30 rue du Bourg, 3960 Sierre   +41 (0)27 456 26 46

The François-Xavier Bagnoud Observatory
High on the slopes overlooking St. Luc known for its clear, calm night-skies; the observatory is open to professional astronomers and curious amateurs alike and makes a beautiful end to an evening. The observatory is accessed with the St. Luc - Tignousa funicular.
+41 (0)27 475 58 08   www.ofxb.ch

Vin du Glacier
Get to know a local and taste the Vin du Glacier. A 400 year old tradition has seen the locals bring wine up from a vineyard in the Rhone Valley and age it close to the glaciers in huge larch barrels.
The tartar on the inside of the barrels is often up to

5 centimetres thick, and the wine is generally aged for at least 25 years, giving it a peculiar taste, unlike any other wine in the world. Each June, the new wine is added to the top of the 500 litre barrels, mixing in with harvests from previous years.

The wine is only used for the private consumption of the locals and is not for sale in shops or restaurants. The trick is to become friendly with a local so as to get an opportunity to try some of this unique beverage that is still being aged in the cellars of about 100 residences in Grimentz. The most extensive selection of glacier wines is kept under the House of Burgesses.

Cheese

Anniviers produces a well refined local alpine cheese which must be sampled.
It is best with a glass of Fendant or Johannisberg.

SPAS AND RELAXATION

"L'eau des Cimes"- Part of "Grand Hôtel Bella Tola"

The alpine spa of the Hotel Bella Tola sits comfortably on the slopes of St. Luc and provides magnificent views across the valley from the terrace - feel the strain ease out of your muscles as you watch the sun going down.

Grand Hôtel Bella Tola & St. Luc, 3961 St. Luc
+41 (0)27 475 14 44   www.bellatola.ch

Züri

Bern

Sion

Val d'anniviers

Zermatt

Geneva

Verbier

Chamonix
Megève
Les Contamines

Monte Rosa

Courmayeur

Val d'Isère/Tignes

Courchevel

Turin

La Grave

Sestriere

TRAVEL

The region is well served by airports with easy looks to Bern, Sion, Zurich and Geneva. As with everywhere else in Switzerland the Val d'Anniviers is well served by public transport, however, due to the dispersed nature of the valley it is most convenient to arrange private transportation.

PUBLIC TRANSPORT

There are direct train services between the valley and Bern, Geneva and Zurich airport every 30 min – the recently opened Lötschberg tunnel gets you there one hour faster.

+41 (0)27 327 35 90   www.valais.ch

Taxi Anniviers Sàrl

A local taxi service that offers both short trips within the valley and flat-rate shuttle services to all the major airports.

+41 (0)79 628 61 11   www.taxianniviers.ch

USEFUL CONTACTS

Sierre-Anniviers Tourism - Regional Tourist Board
  +41 (0)84 884 80 27
  www.sierre-anniviers.ch

Anniviers Guides Office
  +41 (0)27 475 12 00
  www.anniviers-montagne.ch

EMERGENCY NUMBERS
  Sierre Hospital   +41 (0)27 603 70 00

  Sion Hospital   +41 (0)27 603 40 00

"Le Forum",
  Sion Medical Centre   +41 (0)27 329 00 50

VERBIER

Verbier (1,490 m) is the largest ski area in Switzerland, by virtue of its 205 kilometres of pistes. It is a five-star resort for any and all kinds of skiers. Extreme ski aficionados come here, looking for monster moguls and death-defying couloirs.

The Geneva and Paris elite are present as well, enjoying the pistes, the gourmet restaurants and the private parties.

The names of La Tzoumaz, Nendaz, Veysonnaz, Bruson, Les Collons or Thyon are not as well known, but they, together with Verbier, make up the Four Valleys and bring the statistical totals of the entire region to an impressive 400 kilometres of pistes.

SURROUNDINGS

Verbier is one of a handful of resorts that have, through the years, established such a good reputation among off-piste fanatics that it has, by now, become difficult to find much powder without hiking.

To get the goods on one of the classic off-piste routes here, you have to get up very early on the first morning after the first snow has fallen. After day one, hiking is the only option for finding untracked powder.

Chassoure-Tortin (2,740 m)

Mogul skiers will think they have died and gone to heaven when they see this, whereas snowboarders or those not mad about moguls should steer clear of this route if possible.

Mont Fort (3,330 m)

If you like moguls, the face of Mont Fort dishes them out in the size of bunkers. The back side of the mountain has a steep couloir that ultimately leads to an off-piste adventure down to Lac de Cleuson. One of the highest pistes in Europe so the views are not to be missed.

Lac de Cleuson

There is another route to Lac de Cleuson that is accessed with a short hike off to the left of the Col des Gentianes lift.

A great corn snow descent in springtime, this route can be quite dangerous in powder and a guide is imperative.

Stairway to Heaven

This is one of the longtime favourites of Verbier aficionados. A short hike of 20-30 minutes to the left of the Col des Gentianes brings you to the top of a heavenly descent that ultimately brings you to the Tortan restaurant.

Vallon d'Arbi

One reaches this Verbier classic by skiing and traversing below the bottom of the Lac des Vaux lift.

The descent faces north and is a lovely run in between the trees which finishes down in La Tsoumaz so good snow cover is required.

Champs Ferret

A parallel valley to d'Arbi, Champs Ferret requires a reasonable amount of hiking to get into and out of Prarion, but steep powder slopes and tree-skiing are the rewards for the energetic skiers who are willing to walk for their turns.

Mont Gelé

This is Verbier's most extreme mountain. Rarely open nowadays for fear that the plethora of wannabe freeriders who have more guts than skill will put themselves in mortal danger, this is a great mountain with no real pistes. You have to find your own route down amidst an obstacle course of rocks and cliffs.

The Creblet Couloirs

There are four main couloirs ranging in difficulty that begin close to the Attelas peak (2,730 m). As usual in Verbier, a guide is advisable.

Verbier ski season lasts from December until April.

4 Vallées
Mt Fort 3330

Mont Collon
3637 m.

Pigne d'Arolla
3796 m.

Mont-Blanc de Cheilon
5876 m.

La Rusette
3875 m.

Rosablanche
3336 m.

Grande Dissence

Greppon Blanc
2700 m.

L'Etsergeon

Mont-Rouge
3011 m.

Etherolla
2450 m.

Lac de Cleuson

Combatzeline
2238 m.

Tortin
2050 m.

EVOLÈNE
included in Printze
4Vallées

Siviez
1730 m.

THYON 2000
2100 M.

LES MASSES
1515 M.

LES COLLONS
1800 M.

VEYSONNAZ
1400 M.

NENDAZ
1400 M.

MAYENS-DE-L'OURS
1470 M.

Sion

Aproz

MOUNTAINS

MOUNTAIN GUIDES
François Perraudin
Famous photographer and one of the best guides in the area.

+41 (0)796 80 02 33   www.frperraudin.ch

L'École de Ski
At Medran has the best ski instructors.
They also offer heli-ski.

+41 (0)27 775 33 63   www.ecole-de-ski-verbier.ch

EQUIPMENT
Surefoot
A modern clinic for your feet/boots. They make your feet feel like they are directly connected to the edge of your skis.

They also have shops in Courchevel, Val d'Isère and London to name a few.

Le Parador, Rue de Medran, 1936 Verbier   +41 (0)27 771 99 20

RESTAURANTS

MOUNTAIN RESTAURANTS

When visiting some of the huts on the slopes, at some point, one should definitely try croûte au fromage, a local speciality made up of toast drenched in melted cheese and often covered with mushrooms, ham and/or a fried egg. This heavy fare will definitely help replenish some of the energy lost during a morning of hiking and off-piste skiing.

Marmotte
The obvious place on the front of Savoleyres, just below the main drag-lift. They have superb rösti (a rare thing in French-dominated Verbier).
+41 (0)27 771 68 34

Le Namasté
A great all-rounder, in an old hut, on your left descending the front of Savoleyres.
+41 (0)27 771 57 73

Le Carrefour
Located on the Savoleyns side by the main road. When the weather behaves it's a great place to have lunch and enjoy the afternoon sun. We recommend to book a table beforehand on the terrace by the wall. The menu is relaxed and varied — the salads are particularly recommended. Towards the end of the day it usually has a good party atmosphere.
+41 (0)27 771 55 55

Clambin / Chez Dany

A classic, cosy old mountain chalet, in the woods below Ruinettes when going towards Medran (reached by an off-piste skiroute).
+41 (0)27 771 25 24

Cabane Mont Fort

A Verbier classic and a climbing refuge, on the Haute Route tour in a fabulous perched position above La Chaux, hugely popular for its simple (croûtes and polenta) food, whatever the weather. A great terrace and you can stay overnight.
+41 (0)27 778 13 84

RESTAURANTS IN TOWN

La Table d'Adrien

This restaurant at Chalet d'Adrien has a charming relaxed interior and a Michelin starred chef doing top-notch Italian food.

Hotel-Restaurant le Chalet d'Adrien, 1936   +41 (0)27 771 62 00

L'Ecurie

A small traditional restaurant, managed by Lisette with her husband Jean-Marc – "Babouin" – in the kitchen doing excellent grills and regional specialities.

18 carrefour Central, 1936   +41 (0)27 771 27 60

King's

A smart, club-like basement place with excellent, modern, eclectic food. Excellent service with a good Swiss wine list.

Kings Parc Hotel, Rue de la Poste, 1936   +41 (0)27 775 20 35

Le Chaplon

A modern restaurant/bar to the right of Place Centrale. Always a lot of people and the food is quite sophisticated. They also serve food at the bar if you prefer that.

5 chemin des Vernes, 1936   +41 (0)27 771 37 01

APRÈS-SKI

Coco Club
The first luxury VIP club in the Alps. Prepare to spend up big, you can order a cocktail for £5,000!
No expense has been spared on the interior. This is the new place to be, especially for the English.
Place Centrale, 1936   +41 (0)27 771 66 66

Farm Club
An institution in Verbier and, before the arrival of Coco Club used to be "the" place to be seen.
Great atmosphere. Best to book a table for your bottles. Open until 4:00 am or later.
Rue de Verbier, 1936   +41 (0)27 771 61 21

Nevaï
Enjoy an early night drink at the newly renovated Nevaï hotel. It is white/white with a cool fire place. Expensive cocktails although can be lacking in atmosphere.
Rue de Verbier, 1936   +41 (0)27 775 40 40

Le Farinet
Centrally located with live music and a crazy atmosphere. Packed with people inside and out.
Place Centrale, 1936   +41 (0)27 771 66 26

T-bar
Comfortable and lively hang-out. Also a good place for breakfast.
Place Centrale, 1936   +41 (0)27 771 50 07

King's Bar

At the King's Parc hotel, is a laid-back, candlelit cellar bar with a private club atmosphere with great cocktails.

Kings Parc Hotel, Rue de la Poste, 1936   +41 (0)27 775 20 10

Crok No Name

A cool bar with DJs and sometimes live bands. Relaxed and "grown up".

Route de Creux, 1936   +41 (0)27 771 69 34

Fer a cheval

Just below Medran, is good for beer, drinks and pizza. Even with two terraces it gets crammed and often spills onto the street. Favoured by the locals. Breakfast is also available (avant-ski)!

Rue de Médran, 1936   +41 (0)27 771 26 69

HOTELS

Verbier is an unusual ski resort as much of the accommodation here is made up of chalets and there are very few luxury hotels. However, even the lower-end chalets tend to be very nice and some of the high-end chalets border on decadent. If you have a choice and like your sleep, do not stay in the centre of town, as the Farm Club closes at 4:00 am-ish and some of its guests like to sing on their way home!

Chalet d'Adrien

Verbier's only five-star hotel, in a peaceful setting next to the Savoleyres lift base (great views from the terrace and the best rooms). Recently built, in chalet style with an exceptionally welcoming ambience. Neat spa, gym and pool. A seriously refined Italian restaurant. They also offer activities such as horse riding, cookery classes and mountain walks. Even if you choose not to stay here, visit for a meal or a drink.

Chemin des Creux, 1936

+41 (0)27 771 62 00   www.chalet-adrien.com

Montpelier

A quiet hotel slightly out of town where we have stayed a few times. The rooms are fairly basic (please improve!) but the restaurant has outstanding service and food. The pool has a view of the mountains. There is a shuttle bus every morning to the slopes.

Rue de la Piscine, 1936

+41 (0)27 771 61 31   www.hotelmontpelier.ch

Rosalp

It is set to be an après-ski hotspot this season. It's right in the thick of things on the road up to the Medran lifts.

Route de Médran, 1936

+41 (0)27 771 63 23   www.rosalp.com

Nevaï

A modern minimalistic 4-star Alpine hotel with contemporary rooms and a small spa. Top floor suites have their own hot tub on the balcony. Some of the rooms are a little too bare/minimalistic for our taste.

Rue de Verbier, 1936

+41 (0)27 775 40 00   www.nevai.ch

The Lodge Verbier

Sir Richard Branson's mountain retreat available on an exclusive basis only.

A luxurious complex with 9 bedrooms, a 9 m indoor pool, jacuzzi, steam room, spa, party room with large plasma screen and mini ice rink. Meals, drink and chauffeur included.

+44 (0) 20 8600 04 30   www.thelodge.virgin.com

THINGS TO DO

Le Hameau

A modern but traditionally designed cultural complex at the top of the village. Includes an interesting and extensive Alpine museum.

Le Hameau Conference Center, 1936   +41 (0)27 771 75 60

Toboggan run

From the top of Savoleyres to La Tzoumaz – an exceptional 850 m vertical and 10 kilometres long.

SPAS AND RELAXATION

Serious spa

Down in the valley at Lavey les Bains (on the way to Geneva) is an exceptionally impressive spa – a great place to spend a bad-weather day.

Les Bains de Lavey, 1892 Lavey-les-Bains   +41 (0)24 486 15 55

TRAVEL

Verbier is served primarily by Geneva and Zürich airports both of which have easy transport links to the Verbier resort.

PUBLIC TRANSPORT
As ever in Switzerland the train system is probably the fastest and most efficient manner in which to reach your destination.
www.sbb.ch

Taxis and Shuttle Services

Verbier's vast array of taxi firms have been organised
into one main association, this is by far the best place
to turn to for airport links and private services.

+41 (0)79 625 90 85   www.verbiertaxi.ch

USEFUL CONTACTS

Verbier Tourist Office
+41 (0)27 775 38 88
www.verbier.info

Verbier Commune Administration
+41 (0)27 777 11 00
www.bagnes.ch

EMERGENCY NUMBERS
Medical Centre
Dr F. Gay-Crosier   +41 (0)27 771 70 01

OTHER RESORTS

BRUSON

Although not officially part of the extensive 4 Valleys, there are a number of tiny villages nearby that have small lift systems worth a visit.

Bruson, a small town across the valley from Verbier, is an excellent alternative on bad weather days (and a bit of a secret amongst guides).

It has some great tree-skiing which offers visibility and shelter from the wind. In better weather, the top of the bowl above the top lift is accessible with a hike and is also well worth a visit.

Café Le Carrefour

A small country house restaurant (the only house with blue shutters) in the middle of town with excellent food. The homemade blueberry tart was our favourite (isn't it always). Definitely worth a visit.
+41 (0)27 776 14 61

SUPER ST. BERNARD

At the entry to the St. Bernard tunnel, a short drive from Verbier, is the obscure little community of Bourg St. Pierre and the equally unknown Super St. Bernard ski area. The uphill access consists basically of one 750 vertical metre antique lift from 1963 called the Menouve Gondola, but rarely have we seen one lift

access so much skiing. Good off piste skiing abounds on both sides of the lift, and a long off-piste descent to the ski village of Crévacol in Italy is perhaps the true highlight of the area. Check the weather report before coming here, and try the run to Crévacol right after a storm from the south has subsided.

Grand St. Bernard Hospice

Close to Super St. Bernard is the Grand St. Bernard Hospice, a still-active monastery that bred the first St. Bernard dogs to be used for snow rescue. Skiers may stay overnight and eat meals here, using the historic landmark as a base for ski touring, and many pleasant day tours can be done from here. One that

we highly recommend is skiing into Val Feret from the Italian side, a route less travelled that often rewards with 500 m of vertical powder.

+41 (0)27 787 12 36   www.gsbernard.ch

CHAMPEX-LAC

There are only four lifts, but even fewer powder skiers on an average day. One of the lifts is among the steepest in the world.

The way down is by way of a red run, which is no more than a road with one giant hairpin curve, and a very black, unprepared piste to the skier's left of the chairlift. In between is an abundance of ultra-steep tree descents.

ZERMATT

Zermatt (1,610 m) was at the forefront from the beginning, having built the world famous Gornergrat railway in 1898, and opening its first ski school in 1902. It is a legendary venue for skiing.

It has the largest number of high capacity lifts in the world and its 2,200 m vertical drop ranks in the top ten worldwide. Zermatt, however, is much more than just a top 10 resort.

It has charm, beauty, history, and it has soul. All that, and then, there is the Matterhorn!
It is stunning, staggering, stupendous, spectacular, magnificent, awesome and inspirational. It is the perfect mountain - and it does look best from the Swiss side!

SURROUNDINGS

There is so much off-piste to do in and around Zermatt that we can only recommend to ski with a knowledeable guide. To describe it in detail we would need to write a separate book.

With its high altitude, skiing in Zermatt is reliable. Because of its location in the Alps, however, it tends to get mostly smaller snowfalls rather than mega dumps and tends to become better throughout the season.

Sunnegga and Rothorn

Put your skis into overdrive and imitate Franz Klammer on the black National piste under the Blauherd lift,

which has served in the past as a venue for FIS giant slalom races.

The backside of the Rothorn also offers some long delightful runs and when there is enough snow the front of the Rothorn is magnificent.

Gornergrat and Stockhorn

This area affords stupendous views of the Monte Rosa (4,634m) and the Gorner Glacier, and the skiing is also world class. The Gornergrat and the Stockhorn (the last stop above the Gornergrat) offer vast kilometres of steep, north facing slopes off the back side. Part of the area off the back of the Stockhorn is glacial, so

a guide is advised. Don't miss some of the excellent terrain off the sunny side either, with dream views of the Monte Rosa.

Close to the Kelle piste from the Gornergrat, there are various steep off-piste descents between the rocks. These slopes can easily be scouted while skiing in the Sunnegga area, which offers good views of this terrain. Not as easy to scout are the steep pitches and couloirs below the Riffelberg Hotel. These descents are perilously close to sheer cliffs, and you must enlist the service of a guide to find your way around this area.

In between the Gornergrat and the Stockhorn are two additional peaks, Hohtälli and Rote Nase. These both give additional access points to begin off-piste routes down the north faces that end up at Gant. (Remember a helmet to protect your head against the rocks!)

Klein Matterhorn

This is an impressive experience before you even mount your skis. The top cable car takes skiers smack into the sheer cliff face of the Klein Matterhorn. This is one of the better examples of the remarkable Swiss mastery over their mountainous habitat. Mother Nature puts on a show of her own on the way down from the Klein Matterhorn, offering descents through

an obstacle course of blue ice, huge seracs, gaping crevasses, and granite cliffs on the Unterer Theodul Glacier, the Schwarztor Glacier and the Gorner Glacier. The omnipresent Matterhorn looms over the entire scene giving skiers the constant feeling of being close to the Creator. Always ski with a guide in glacial terrain.

Schwarzsee

The Hermetji, Tiefbach and Momatt black pistes, plus a few kilometres of steep tree-skiing in between these routes provide some of our favourite skiing in Zermatt. These are not ordinary black pistes – in fact one of them, the Momatt descent, cannot be opened early in the season, as the frozen waterfall in the guts of the gully must first be covered with enough snow to render it skiable!

Skiing in Zermatt runs from mid-December until mid-April.

Mountain peaks and locations labelled on the map:

Monte Rosa
Dufourspitze 4634
Liskamm 4527
Breithorn 4164
Matterhorn
Rimpfischhorn 4199
Strahlhorn 4190
Cima di Jazzi 3803
Stockhorn 3405
Monte Rosa Hütte 2795
Rote Nase 3247
Hohtälli 3286
Gornergletscher
Gandegghütte 3030
Rothorn paradise 3103
Fluhalp 2616
Triftji 2715
Rosenritz 3006
Gornergrat 3089
Trockener Steg 2939
Kumme 2775
Blauherd 2571
Gifthittli 2935
Sandiger Bo 2786
Gant 2223
Grünsee 2300
Breitboden 2514
Rotenboden 2815
Projekt 2010
NEU
Sunnegga paradise 2288
Riffelberg 2582
Findeln
Riffelalp 2211
Landtunnel
Tuftern 2216
Schwarzsee paradise 2583
Patrullarve 2000
Furgg 2432
Ried
Findelbach 1774
Furi 1864
Zum See
Blatten
Stafel 2199
Zermatt 1620
Zmutt 1936
Projekt 2010

Legend:

| Bahnen / Transports / Transports / Trenino | leichte Piste / Easy pistes / Piste facile / Pista facile | mittelschwere Piste / Medium pistes / Piste moyen / Pista media | schwierige Piste / Difficult pistes / Piste difficile / Pista difficile | Piste beschneit oder Gletscher / Piste with snowmaking / Piste enneigement artificiel ou glacier / Pista ad innevamento programmato | Abfahrtsrouten / Itinéraires ski runs / Itinéraires à ski / Piste di discesa | Winterwanderweg / Walking paths / Sentiers de randonnée / Sentiero da trekking invernale | Schlitte / Sledge / Piste pe / Pista da |

MOUNTAINS

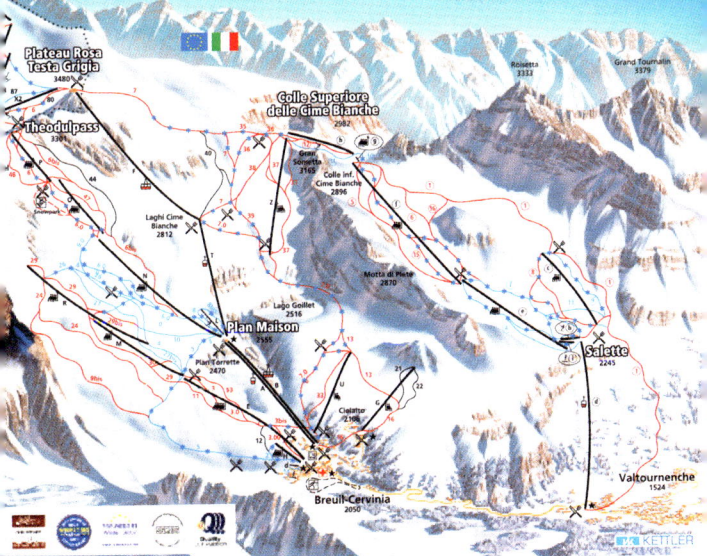

Rothorn paradise
1 Unterer Rothorn
2 Ried
3 Riedweg
4 Brunnjischbord
5 Eisfluh
6 Easy run
7 Standard
8 Obere National
9 Tuftern
10 Paradise
11 Rotweng
12 Schneefluh
13 Oberhill
14 Kumme
15 Tufternkurasse
16 Chamois

17 Marmotte
18 Arbzug
19 Fluhalp
20 Rio
21 Gant - Findeln

Gornergrat
24 Berize
25 Grünsee
26 Bahnbrunnen
28 White Hare
29 Kelle
30 Mittelritz
31 Platte
32 Grieschumre
33 Trifti
34 Stockhorn

35 Gifinnti
36 Gornergrat
37 Riffelhorn
38 Rotenboden
39 Riffelalp
40 Riffelboden
41 Landtunnel
42 Schweignatten
43 Moos
44 Hohtälli

Matterhorn glacier paradise
Schwarzsee paradise
49 Rietli
50 Blatten
51 Weisse Perle
52 Stafelalp

53 Oberer Tiefbach
54 Hörnli
55 Höfi
56 Kuhbodmen
57 Ambeld
58 Furgg
61 Tiefbach
62 Momatt
64 Skiweg
6a Furgg - Furi
6b Sandiger Boden
64 Garten
65 Rennststrecke
66 Theodulsee
67 Garten Bucketpiste
68 Tunnigo
69 Matterhorn

70 Schneepiste
71 Theodulgletscher
72 Furggsattel
73 Gandegg
74 Gandegghütte

Sommerski Theodulgletscher
80 Testa Grigia
81 Fürregletsk
82 Mittelpiste
83 Plateau Rosa
84 Ventina Glacier
8c Matterhorn Glacierparadise
86 Gobba di Rollin
87 Verbindungspiste

Total Pisten
Matterhorn ski paradise   313 km
Beschneite Pisten oder
auf Gletscher   60%

SOS Pistenrettungsdienst Zermatt Bergbahnen: Tel. +41 (0) 27 966 01 01

-grenze	Sommerski	Wild- und Waldschutzgebiet - bei Missachtung Skipasszug	Anfänger-Park
al boundary	Summer skiing	Forest and wildlife protected areas - revocation of the skipass in case of disregarding	Park for beginners
re nationale	Ski d'été	Zone de protection de la forêt et de la faune - non-respect, retrait le skipass sans compensation	Domaine pour les débutants
nazionale	Sci estivo	Riserva boschiva e faunistica - comporta l'immediato ritiro del skipass	Spazio per principianti

Gletscher-Palast
Glacier palace
Palais de glace
Palazzo di ghiaccio

MOUNTAIN GUIDES
Jan Adventures
Jan Schnidrig is a very good guide for off-piste and heli-skiing in Zermatt. He also does tours to Gudauri, Greenland.

+41 (0)78 606 34 62   www.janadventures.ch

Christoph Petrig
Has become a good friend and is an inspirational ski and mountain guide who knows every nook of the mountains. You can also stay at his City Hotel Garni.

+41 (0)27 966 39 40   www.cityzermatt.com

EQUIPMENT
Anorak
Quality mountain gear to buy or hire including Patagonia and Black Diamond.

20 Bahnhofstrasse, 3920   +41 (0)27 968 17 77

Bayard Sport & Fashion
Have a main shop at the station and four shops on the main street. Telemark and alpine ski rental. They stock hand-made Swiss skis from Stockli, also Zai, Mammut and Kjus. A good range of equipment and friendly service.

+41 (0)27 966 49 50   www.bayardzermatt.ch

RESTAURANTS

Zermatt is one of the few places in the world where you can be served a perfect, homemade al dente chantarelle risotto with a glass of Billecart-Salmon Rosé for lunch.
We recommend you book restaurants in advance – both on the mountain and for dinner.

MOUNTAIN RESTAURANTS
SUNNEGGA
Fluhalp

Off to the left when you ski from Rothorn. Great Swiss/Italian food and wine.

Book a table outside if it is not too cold, otherwise we prefer to sit upstairs. It normally has live music as well.

+41 (0)27 967 25 97   www.fluhalp-zermatt.ch

Tufternalp

An old hut on the tree-line in the Sunnegga sector; it offers a superb Matterhorn view and simple mountain food (sausages and cheese slices). You may see deer feeding nearby.

16 Steinmattstrasse, 3920   +41 (0)27 967 54 95

FINDELN
Findeln is a scattering of wooden chalets below Sunnegga sharing fabulous Matterhorn views.
Chez Vrony (2,100 m)

A charming old chalet with a sophisticated, if sometimes

a tad too creative, mountain menu, impeccable service, a hip feel and a big terrace.

+41 (0)27 967 25 52   www.chezvrony.ch

Findlerhof

Smaller than Chez Vrony but is a good alternative with an excellent menu and great service. Early in the season you may want to book inside as there is only limited sun on the terrace.

+41 (0)27 967 25 88   www.findlerhof.ch

GORNERGRAT
Hotel Riffelberg

A charming place for a hot chocolate or a lunch on the outside terrace. The food has improved tremendously over the years.

+41 (0)27 966 65 00

Igloo Bar

Stop for a coffee or drink to experience the unique Igloo Bar in the Igloo village, which is rebuilt each year. Go on a Tuesday for the gourmet fondue.

+41 (0)41 612 27 28   www.iglu-dorf.com

KLEIN MATTERHORN
Zum See

Off the home run from Furi and the Glacier sector. This is a fantastic restaurant with masses of ambience and a really excellent and sophisticated

menu. Don't come home from Zermatt without having
been here — in our book it ranks up with the top five
mountain restaurants in the Alps.
+41 (0)27 967 20 45

Gandegghütte

Off the beaten track at 3,030 m, above Trockener Steg.
It serves simple mountain food and offers fantastic
views.
+41 (0)79 607 88 68

Bergrestaurant Blatten

Further down from Zum See, a very cosy, two storey hut
with a terrace in the sun. Their local food is fantastic.
Early in the season the sun only lasts until 1:30 pm on
the terrace.
+41 (0)27 967 20 96

Rifugio Guide del Cervino

A mountain hut on the Swiss-Italian watershed in Plateau
Rosà 3,480 m, giving it fantastic views, especially
at sunset and sunrise. Hearty Italian food.
+39 (0)16 694 83 69

RESTAURANTS IN TOWN

Le Gitan

A cosy restaurant with an open fire where succulent lamb is roasted as you wait. A good and varied wine list. Don't be put off by the uncharming entrance.

Le Gitan-Zermatterstübli, 64 Bahnhofstrasse, 3920
+41 (0)27 968 19 40

The Pipe

A trendy little "surfers' cantina" doing innovative food with Asian, African and Caribbean influences.

38 Kirchstrasse, 3920 +41 (0)79 758 53 24

Heimberg (once Mood's)

An innovative bar/restaurant/wine shop – the latest venture of Heinz Julen (of the Vernissage).

84 Bahnhofstrasse, 3920 +41 (0)27 967 84 84

Restaurant Lusi

At Grand Hotel Zermatterhof has a young and modern atmosphere.

It offers light cuisine with a Mediterranean touch in an alpine environment. When the sun comes into the valley it is a perfect place to sit on the terrace.

55 Bahnhofstrasse, 3920
+41 27 966 66 00 www.zermatterhof.ch/lusi.html

APRÈS-SKI

BLATTEN AND ZUM SEE

Part way down the mountain between Furi and Zermatt, when descending from the Schwarzsee ski area, are cosy hamlets of old farmhouses in Blatten and Zum See.

Either on the sunny terraces in spring or indoors on a cold winter afternoon, there is no better location to begin your après-ski activities (see Mountain Restaurants).

Elsie's

An ancient, cosy little chalet that has been serving Champagne and oysters (fresh daily) for decades.

16 Kirchplatz, 3920   +41 (0)27 967 24 31

Snowboat

Near the Sunnegga lift.
It has good coffee and sandwiches during the day
and an in and outdoor bar in the afternoon.
20 Vispastrasse, 3920 +41 (0)27 967 43 33

Vernissage

A cool glass-and-steel affair, incorporating an art
gallery and a cinema (projection room open to view).
Also check out the same owner's modish new
Heimberg (see Restaurants.)
4 Hofmattstrasse, 3920 +41 (0)27 967 66 36

Hotel Post

A Zermatt institution and recently updated quite
smartly. It is a warren of bars, restaurants and a disco
that includes a cosy lounge bar (Papa Caesar) and a
live music bar (The Pink).
41 Bahnhofstrasse, 3920 +41 (0)27 967 19 31

NIGHTCLUBS

Schneewittchen

Schneewittchen is beneath the ever-popular Papperla
Pub après-ski bar.
Other nightclubs to mention are The Broken and Le
Village in the hotel Post (see above).
34 Steinmattstrasse, 3920 +41 (0)79 220 79 14

HOTELS

Riffelalp Resort 2,222 m

Our favourite hotel in Zermatt and possibly one of the best hotels in the Alps.

This is a five-star luxury chalet-style hotel just above the tree-line (first stop on the Gornergrat railway, with the last train at 11:30 pm).

It offers impeccable service, glorious Matterhorn views (of course), Toblerone fondues, cinema, a large humidour and an outdoor heated pool.

You have to book years (literally) in advance to secure a room here.

+41 (0)27 966 05 55   www.riffelalp.com

Mont Cervin Palace

Is truly palatial; the biggest in town, elegantly traditional, with a good pool and a new wellness centre with a miracle back treatment - massage and electric "shocks".

31 Bahnhofstrasse, 3920

+41 (0)27 966 88 88   www.seilerhotels.ch/mont-cervin-palace

The Omnia

A cutting-edge member of the "design hotels" group, with a super-cool, if somewhat static, interior and furniture from big-name American and European designers (lots of granite). It's perched above the village centre and reached by tunnel and lift.

Auf dem Fels, 3920

+41 (0)27 966 71 71   www.the-omnia.com

Romantik Hotel Julen

A sophisticated modern chalet across the river from the centre.
Wood-panelled rooms and romantic chic-rustic decor.
2 Riedstrasse, 3920
+41 (0)27 966 76 00   www.julen.com

Cœur des Alpes

A fabulous little b&b hotel close to the Klein Matterhorn lifts stylish, warm and great service.
Ask for a Matterhorn view.
Oberdorfstrasse, 3920
+41 (0)27 966 40 80   www.coeurdesalpes.ch

Hotel Firefly

A new and welcome addition to Zermatt, the Hotel Firefly is an elegant combination of alpine heritage and modern chic. Though the hotel is new, the 'DuPont' restaurant is over 200 years old and has remained in the Kalbermatter family throughout.
55 Schluhmattstrasse, 3920
+41 (0)27 967 76 76   www.firefly-zermatt.ch

THINGS TO DO

The Gornergrat Railway

The cogwheel train was the first form of transport for skiers, and this functioning museum piece is proof that uphill transport can also be part of the entertainment on a ski vacation.

The trip takes a full 40 minutes so bring a beer and a sandwich and enjoy the Swiss scenery unfolding outside your window while you imagine what skiing was like a hundred years ago. Sit on the right for Matterhorn views.

20 Nordstrasse, 3900 Brig
+41 (0)27 921 47 11
www.gornergrat.ch

Toboggan runs

There are two short ones: Rotenboden to Riffelberg (drink hot chocolate in the Riffelberg Hotel) and Furi to Zermatt on Tuesday and Thursday evenings only. And there's one big 600 m vertical one: Sunnegga via Findeln to Zermatt on Wednesday evenings only.

Long walks

There are beautiful long walks from Zermatt (45 km of cleared trails). One of the best, taking about 90 min, is to Zmutt, where the Jägerstube does fine rösti and strüdel.

Glacier Palace

See the glacier from the inside: at the Glacier Palace on Klein Matterhorn. Stay overnight in the Igloo Village at Rotenboden, at 2,800m (reached by the Gornergrat railway) with multi-bed 'dormitory' igloos or 'romantic' igloos for two. The guides at the Alpin Center organise ice climbing by the day, in groups or one-to-one. +41 (0) 41 612 27 28

TRAVEL

*Zermatt is well placed as far as airports are concerned
with Zurich, Basel, Geneva and Milan airports all around
three to four hours away by car.*
*The town itself is fully pedestrianised with private
vehicles only permitted as far as Täsch, around 5 km
form Zermatt, where are plenty of parking facilities and
regular shuttle services to the town itself.*

PUBLIC TRANSPORT
Train
The most practical route to Zermatt from any airport
is by rail, the recently opened Lötschberg tunnel
having reduced travel time by up to an hour for many
routes.
www.sbb.ch

USEFUL CONTACTS

Zermatt Tourism
+41 (0)27 966 81 00
www.zermatt.ch

Zermatt Alpine Centre
+41 (0)27 966 24 60
www.alpincenter-zermatt.ch

Zermatt Berbahnen AG
Ski lift and piste information
+41 (0)27 966 01 01
www.matterhornparadise.ch

EMERGENCY NUMBERS
Air Ambulance
+41 (0)27 966 86 86

NATIONAL EMERGENCY NUMBERS

European Emergency Phone Number	112
Police	117
Fire services	118
Ambulance	144
Swiss Air-Rescue, Rega	1414

Whilst we would love to spend every day
of the season skiing in each resort,
we just don't have the time!

Therefore we welcome any comments,
suggestions or feedback from you.

Please email skiguide@lindewerdelin.com

— • —

Credits

Sierre-Anniviers Tourism - Verbier St-Bernard
Zermatt Tourisme - Bodega Misani
Brupbacher SA / Hotel Montpelier Verbier - Chesa Dorta
El Paradiso - Heimburg - Hotel Bela Tola & St-Luc SA
Hotel Castel - Hotel Mont Cervin / Seiler Hotels Zermatt AG
Hotel Misani - Hotel Nevaï - Hotel Survetta
Iglu Bar / iglu-dorf.com - Istockphoto - Kings Park
R. Mathis - Observatoire François-Xavier Bagnoud
Tzambron - Vernissage - X. Christen - J. Condron
Davidson - J. Hadik - A. Mettler / swiss-image.ch
F. Moscatello - Müller - T. Sterchi - T. Talent - Tschuggen
Hotel Group AG / Carlton Hotel
Weibel Communication AG / Bodega Misani

Illustrations Dominique Bertail / module-etrange.com

iPhone® is a trademark of Apple Inc.

**Beautiful
Books**

First published 2009

Beautiful Books Limited
36-38 Glasshouse Street
London W1B 5DL

www.beautiful-books.co.uk

ISBN 9781905636754

Copyright © Morten Linde and Jorn Werdelin 2009

— • —

A catalogue reference for this book
is available from the British Library

— • —